A PLUME BOOK

T-REX TRYING

HUGH MURPHY is a student at the University of Southern California, Ostrow School of Dentistry.

T-REX TRYING...

Hugh Murphy

A PLUME BOOK

PLUME
Published by Penguin Group
Penguin Group (USA) Inc., 375 Hudson Street, New York, New York 10014, U.S.A. • Penguin Group (Canada), 90 Eglinton Avenue East, Suite 700, Toronto, Ontario, Canada M4P 2Y3 (a division of Pearson Penguin Canada Inc.) • Penguin Books Ltd., 80 Strand, London WC2R 0RL, England • Penguin Ireland, 25 St. Stephen's Green, Dublin 2, Ireland (a division of Penguin Books Ltd.) • Penguin Group (Australia), 707 Collins Street, Melbourne, Victoria 3008, Australia (a division of Pearson Australia Group Pty. Ltd.) • Penguin Books India Pvt. Ltd., 11 Community Centre, Panchsheel Park, New Delhi – 110 017, India • Penguin Books (NZ), 67 Apollo Drive, Rosedale, Auckland 0632, New Zealand (a division of Pearson New Zealand Ltd.) • Penguin Books, Rosebank Office Park, 181 Jan Smuts Avenue, Parktown North 2193, South Africa • Penguin China, B7 Jiaming Center, 27 East Third Ring Road North, Chaoyang District, Beijing 100020, China

Penguin Books Ltd., Registered Offices: 80 Strand, London WC2R 0RL, England

First published by Plume, a member of Penguin Group (USA) Inc.

First Printing, February 2013
10 9 8 7 6 5 4 3

Copyright © Hugh Murphy, 2013
All rights reserved

Some illustrations previously appeared on the author's blog, http://trextrying.tumblr.com.

Ⓟ REGISTERED TRADEMARK—MARCA REGISTRADA

ISBN 978-0-452-29902-3

Printed in the United States of America

For Sarah—the brightest, best, most beautiful person in my life

T-Rex trying to paint his house...

T-Rex trying to pull out a trundle bed...

T-Rex trying to hang X-mas ornaments . . .

T-Rex trying to pick flowers . . .

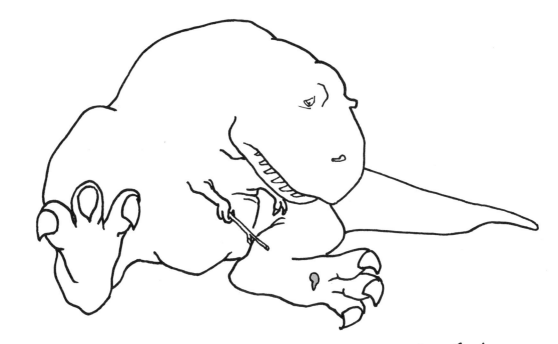

T-Rex trying to get gum off the bottom of his foot...

T-Rex trying to make snow angels...

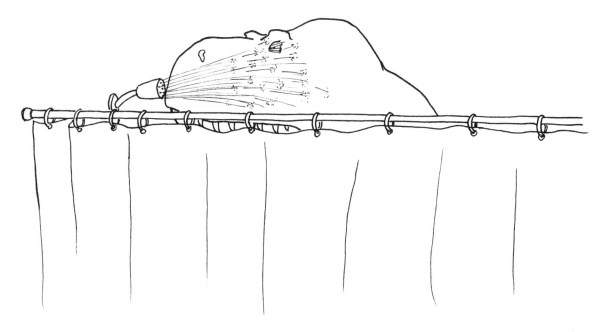

T-Rex trying to adjust the shower head. . .

T-Rex trying to steal from a
vending machine...

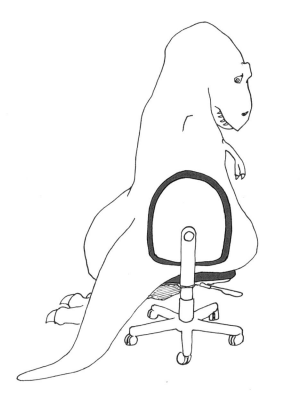

T-Rex trying to adjust his office chair...

T-Rex trying to ask for a new roll of toilet paper from the next stall . . .

T-Rex trying to do a cartwheel...

T-Rex tryin' to put on a cardigan

T-Rex trying to make some alterations to his cardigan . . .

T-Rex trying to use the speed bag...

T-Rex trying to clean his ears with a Q-tip...

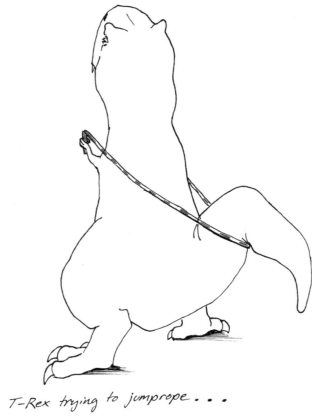

T-Rex trying to jumprope...

T-Rex trying to compete in a wheelbarrow race . . .

T-Rex trying to use a buffet with a sneeze guard...

T-Rex trying to get the prize out of a cereal box. . . .

T-Rex trying to spin the wheel on The Price is Right . . .

T-Rex trying to fold a map...

12 FT

T-Rex trying to use Water Wings . . .

T-Rex trying to get into the attic...

T-Rex trying batting practice . . .

T-Rex trying to start a curling team...

T-Rex trying to play volleyball...

T-Rex trying to paddle a canoe

T-Rex trying to climb a tree. . .

T-REX trying to do a trust fall . . .

T-Rex trying to use a hand dryer in a public restroom. . .

T-Rex trying to use a drive thru ATM...

T-Rex trying to throw his hat at graduation . . .

T-Rex trying downward-dog...

T-Rex trying to play with a sparkler...

T-Rex trying to build a ship in a bottle . . .

T-Rex trying to ribbon dance . . .

T-Rex trying to cross-country ski . . .

T-Rex trying to use eye drops . . .

T-Rex trying to change the
batteries in his smoke detector...

T-Rex trying to play rock-paper-scissors...

T-Rex trying to get to the bottom of a can of chips...

T-Rex trying to squeegee his windshield . . .

T-Rex trying to ride a horse...

T-Rex trying to play the bongos...

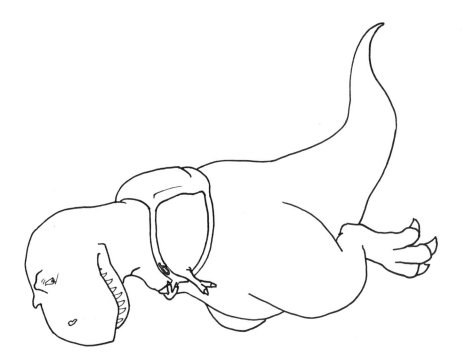

T-Rex trying to pull the ripcord on his parachute . . .

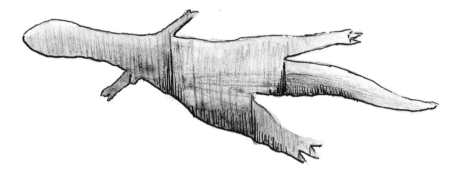

T-Rex trying to hang glide...

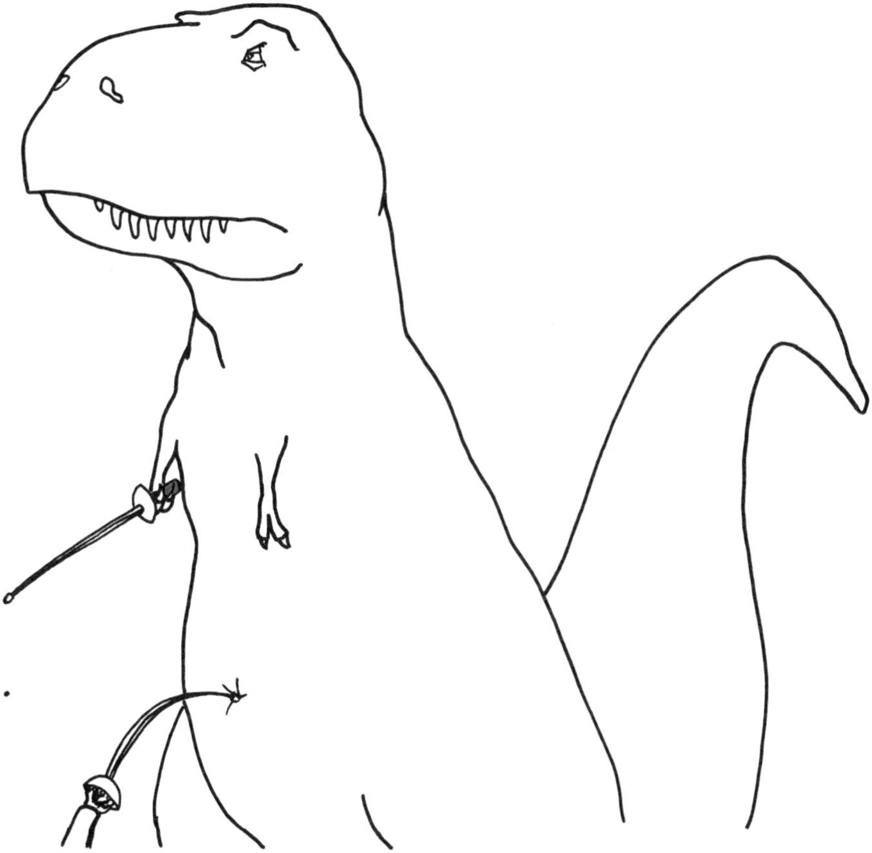

T-Rex trying fencing...

T-Rex trying sock puppets. . .

T-Rex trying to write a screenplay . . .

T-Rex trying to do a wine tasting . . .

T-Rex trying to bag groceries . . .

T-Rex trying to tightrope walk . . .

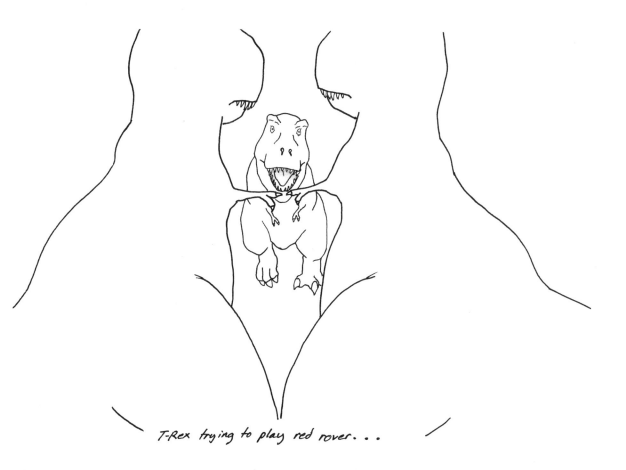

T-Rex trying to play red rover. . .

T-Rex trying to play a round of golf . . .

T-Rex trying to hitchhike . . .

T-Rex trying to make balloon animals . . .

T-Rex trying to clean the litter box . . .

T-Rex trying to shuffle a deck of cards . . .

T-Rex trying to rock climb . . .

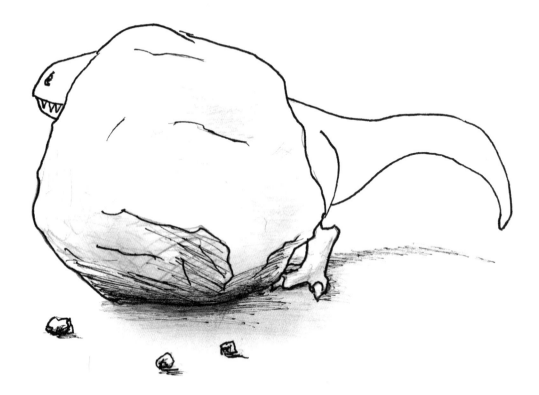

T-Rex trying to play hide & seek . . .

T-Rex trying to sing head, shoulders, knees and toes . . .

T-Rex trying to send a letter...

T-Rex trying the javelin . . .

T-Rex trying to change a light bulb...

T-Rex trying to win at an auction...

Chopsticks

T-Rex trying to play the piano...

T-Rex trying to play tetherball...

T-Rex trying to paint a self-portrait...

T-Rex trying to hang a painting . . .

T-Rex trying to hang curtains...

T-Rex trying to play the harp...

T-Rex trying to turn off a ceiling fan...

T-Rex trying to brush his teeth . . .

T-Rex trying to floss...

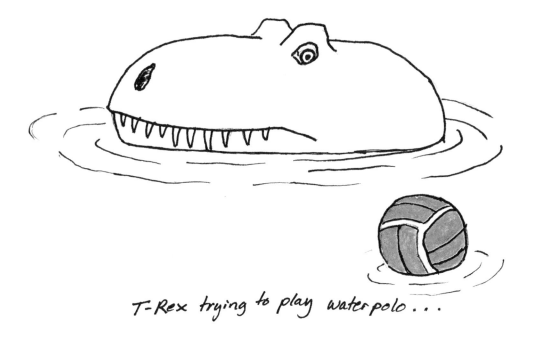

T-Rex trying to play waterpolo...

T-Rex tryin' to play the flute...

T-Rex trying to land a fish . . .

T-Rex trying to brag about the fish he caught...

T-Rex trying to rescue a cat from a tree . . .

T-Rex trying to recline his La-Z-Boy...

T-Rex trying to catch a frisbee...

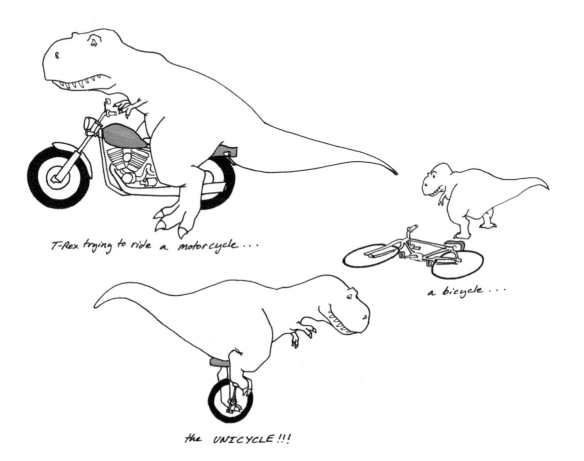

T-Rex trying to ride a motorcycle...

a bicycle...

the UNICYCLE!!!

T-Rex trying to pump up the tire on his unicycle . . .

T-Rex trying to clean his gutters...

T-Rex trying to take up photography. . .

T-Rex trying to get a round of pints from the bar...

T-Rex trying to use bellows to start a fire . . .

T-Rex trying to roast a marshmallow . . .

T-Rex trying to design a skyscraper. . .

T-Rex trying to play the parachute game...

T-Rex trying to play pinball . . .

T-Rex trying to be king of the world...

TITANIC

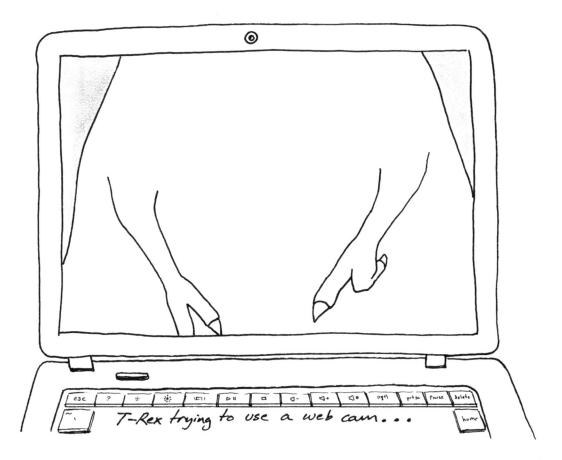

T-Rex trying to use a web cam . . .

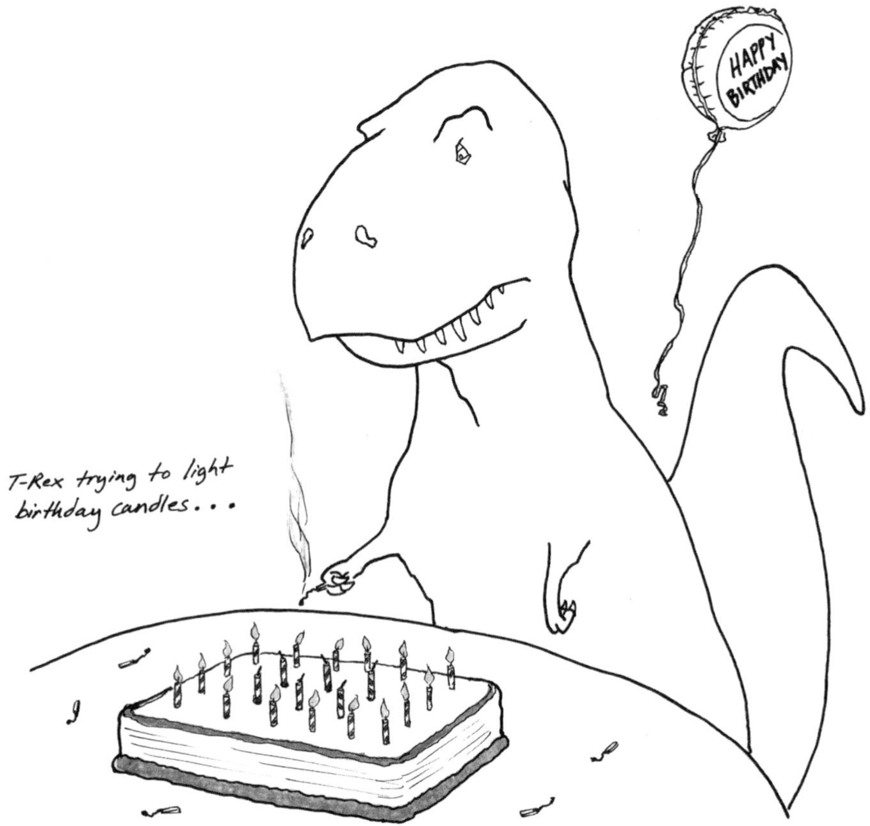
HAPPY BIRTHDAY
T-Rex trying to light birthday candles . . .

T-Rex trying to play paintball...

T-Rex trying to cross his arms in discontent. . .

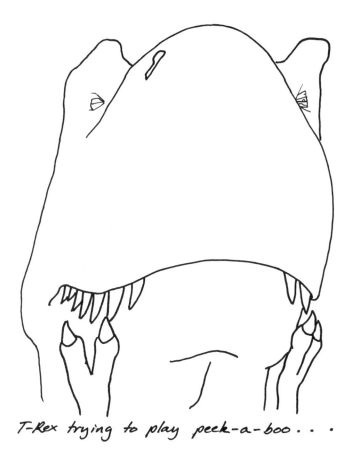

T-Rex trying to play peek-a-boo...

T-Rex trying bird watching . . .

T-Rex trying to use an umbrella...

T-Rex trying to watch a movie in 3D . . .

T-Rex trying to climb the monkey bars. . .

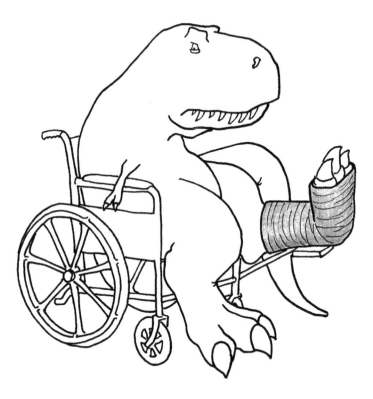

T-Rex trying to use a wheelchair . . .

T-Rex trying to use a table saw . . .

T-Rex trying to chart exponential growth . . .

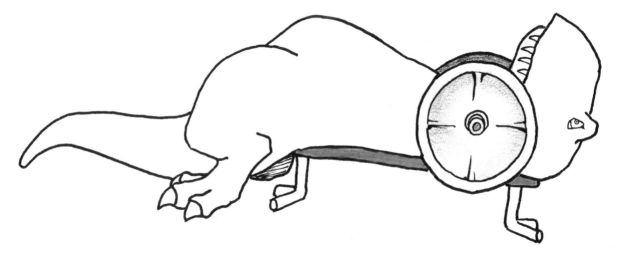

T-Rex trying to bench press . . .

T-Rex trying to start a lawn mower . . .

T-Rex trying to retrieve his keys from a storm drain...

T-Rex trying falconry...

T-Rex trying to buy skinny jeans . . .

T-Rex trying to get a custom-made suit. . .

T-Rex trying to look after a flock of sheep . . .

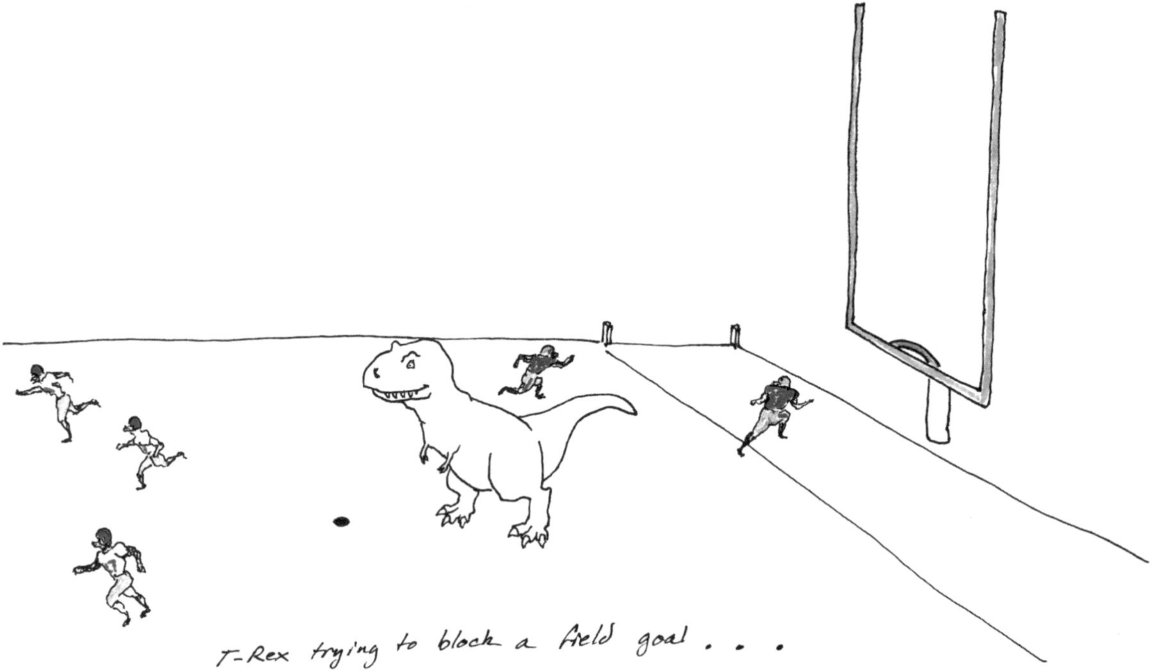

T-Rex trying to block a field goal . . .

T-Rex trying to milk a cow...

T-Rex trying to work at L.A.X. . . .

T-Rex trying to DJ a turntable . . .

T-Rex trying...

T-Rex trying to pin the tail on the donkey...

T-Rex trying to count to five...

T-Rex trying to hit a piñata...

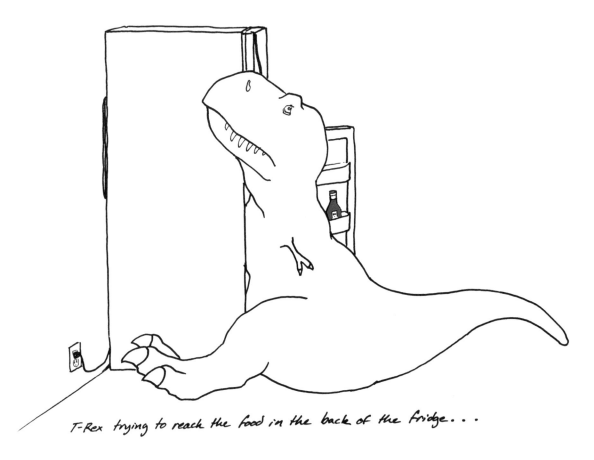

T-Rex trying to reach the food in the back of the fridge . . .

T-Rex trying to use sunscreen...

T-Rex trying to play the bass...

the banjo...

the UKULELE!!!